THE MONSTER MONEY BOOK

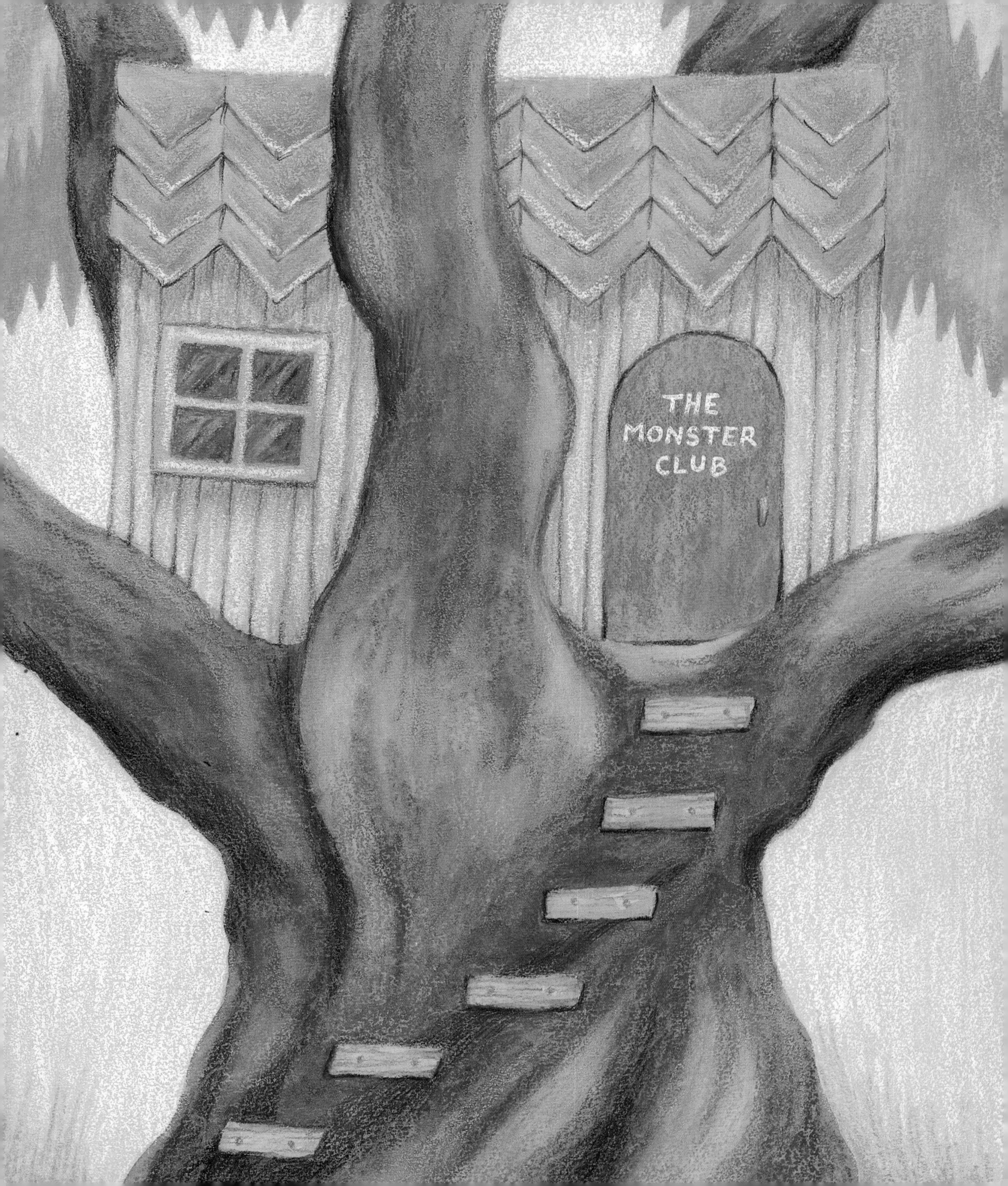
THE
MONSTER
CLUB

THE
MONSTER MONEY BOOK

written and illustrated by Loreen Leedy

Holiday House   New York

For Greg

Library of Congress Cataloging-in-Publication Data
Leedy, Loreen.
    The monster money book / written and illustrated by Loreen Leedy.
    —1st ed.
      p.   cm.
    Summary: The members of the Monster Club discuss what to do with
the fifty-four dollars in their treasury.
    ISBN 0-8234-0922-8
    [1. Money—Fiction. 2. Clubs—Fiction. 3. Monsters—Fiction.]
I. Title.
PZ7.L51524Mo   1992   91-18168   CIP   AC
[E]—dc20
   ISBN 0-8234-1558-9 (pbk.)

More than anything in the world, Grub wanted to join The Monster Club. So he went to talk to his brother Spots, who was the president.

The next day, Sarah and Grub met the other members at the clubhouse.

The meeting began.

Let's start with the treasurer's report.

We have $54.00. Here are my numbers.

penny

nickel

dime

quarter

100 pennies = 1 dollar

20 nickels = 1 dollar

10 dimes = 1 dollar

4 quarters = 1 dollar
_____
coins   4 dollars

10 ones   = 10 dollars

2 fives   = 10 dollars

1 ten   = 10 dollars

1 twenty   = 20 dollars
_____
bills   50 dollars

$4.00 + $50.00 = ($54.00)

Let's think of ways to spend money that will help the club!

How about paint for the clubhouse?

Wood for new steps!

A refrigerator!

Sarah stood up to ask a question.

If you *invest* money in lemons and sugar, then sell lots of lemonade, you can make more money than what you started with.

The extra money is called a profit.

EXPENSES = $10.00

40 glasses × 50¢ = $20.00
expenses − $10.00
PROFIT $10.00

Oh, we did that for our car wash. We bought sponges and soap and wax and washed lots of cars. We made a profit of $20.00.

Spots held up his paw.

I've got another idea. Let's *give* some money away.

Why would we want to do that?

We could give money to someone who really needs it.

If we give money to a good cause, it will make the neighborhood better for all of us.

FOOD DONATIONS
THANK YOU!

CLEAN THE EARTH

RECYCLE

PLEASE GIVE

CARING
FOR
CRITTERS

I really need some money!

I said a *good* cause.

Money in the bank earns interest.

How interesting.

It is!

If you put $100.00 in a piggy bank at home, a year later you will still have $100.00.

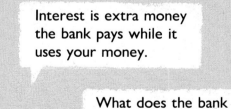

If you put $100.00 in a bank savings account that pays 5% interest, a year later you will have $105.00.

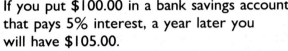

Interest is extra money the bank pays while it uses your money.

What does the bank use our money for?

The bank lends money to people who need it. For example, someone might borrow money to buy a new house.

My parents write checks instead of using cash.

How do you write a check?

When you put money in a checking account, the bank gives you blank checks.

To spend money, you fill out a check and sign your name.

The money comes out of your account and goes to the person or group to whom you wrote the check.

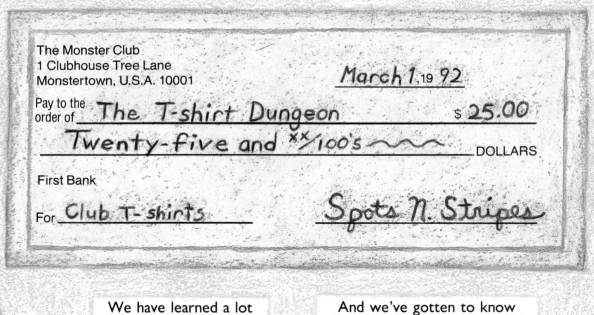

The Monster Club
1 Clubhouse Tree Lane
Monstertown, U.S.A. 10001

March 1, 19 92

Pay to the order of ___The T-shirt Dungeon___ $ 25.00

___Twenty-five and ˣˣ/100's___ DOLLARS

First Bank

For ___Club T-shirts___ ___Spots N. Stripes___

We have learned a lot about money today.

And we've gotten to know Grub and Sarah better, too!

The club members had one more thing to do.

GLOSSARY

Allowance: a sum of money received regularly, often once a week.

Bill: a piece of paper money.

Borrow: to receive money that will be paid back in the future.

Budget: a plan for using money.

Cash: paper money and coins.

Check: a printed piece of paper that, when filled out, allows one to withdraw money from a checking account.

Checking account: a sum of money placed in a bank by a person or group, which is spent when a check is written.

Coin: a small, flat, round piece of metal used as money.

Debt: an amount of money owed to a lender.

Donation: a gift of money to a person or group.

Dues: a sum of money paid to an organization by its members.

Earn: to receive money, usually for work.

Expense: how much something costs.

Interest: the extra money a bank pays a customer for the use of his or her funds.

Invest: to use money to make more money.

Lend: to provide money that must be paid back in the future.

Money: the coins and bills made by the government for people to trade for goods and services.

Price: the sum of money charged for a product or service.

Profit: the money left over after expenses have been paid.

Save: to keep money for future use, instead of spending it right away.

Savings account: a sum of money that earns interest from the bank.

Spend: to pay money for something.

Treasurer: the person who takes care of money for a group.

Withdraw: to remove money from a bank account.